THE EMPATH'S SELF-CARE JOURNAL

This journal belongs to

_____

THE EMPATH'S SELF-CARE JOURNAL

52 Weeks of Prompts,
Practices, and
Positive Affirmations
to Help You Thrive

Mishka Clavijo Kimball, MS, LMFT

ROCKRIDGE
PRESS

To my grandfather Coco,
my husband Paul,
my parents, and my family.

————————————————

To all the beautiful, sensitive
souls who are changing the world
one person at a time.

Contents

Introduction

Dear Empaths, welcome to your self-care journal! My name is Mishka Clavijo Kimball. I am a Latina, a licensed marriage and family therapist, a life coach, and an intuitive, physical, and emotional Empath. I have a master's degree in psychology and more than eight years of experience working in the field of mental health. I run a private practice in Los Angeles, California, where I specialize in helping Empaths and Highly Sensitive adults heal and transform from the inside out. I utilize a holistic approach that focuses on body, mind, and spirit and believe that every person has the potential to overcome obstacles and live a life of balance and harmony.

I was always a little different, an "old soul" from a very young age. I grew up believing that I was "too sensitive" and that I needed to toughen up. As a teenager and young adult, I experienced anxiety, depression, low self-esteem, and self-doubt. One day I made a discovery that would completely change the way I thought of myself. I learned that there was nothing wrong with me. Yes, I was different because I had a gift: I was an Empath.

What is an Empath? First, each Empath is unique. There is only one YOU.

An Empath is a person who is highly in tune with their surroundings, such as the emotions, physical sensations, and/or energy of other people, animals, plants, and nature. Empaths are also highly intuitive and highly empathic. However, being an Empath is not the same as having empathy. Empaths go beyond the ability to understand others' emotions or experiences, because they can feel what others are feeling within their own soul and body. Again, not every Empath is the same, so it is important that you explore your own gifts and abilities.

My goal in writing this journal is to provide a space for YOU to grow, heal, transform, and thrive as an Empath. This journal is meant to help you improve your self-care practices so that you can feel happier, more at peace, and more energized each day.

The journal includes 52 positive affirmations, prompts, and practices to help you incorporate self-care in your daily life. It is meant to be used as a guide throughout the year. You may follow the journal in order, by completing one page per week, or you can choose to use it any way you prefer.

As you embark on this self-care journey, my wish for you is that you live your life as a thriving Empath knowing that you have a powerful and special gift and that you can live a life full of peace and joy.

Empath Self-Care Basics

Growing up in Latinx culture, I never heard the term self-care. In fact, I didn't learn what self-care was until I was in graduate school. I remember being in class and my professor asked, "How is your self-care?" I had no idea what she was talking about until she explained it and said that self-care was essential for our survival and well-being. This is when I learned that self-care is a conscious and intentional decision to improve our mental, emotional, spiritual, social, and physical well-being. Self-care is also self-love, self-reflection, and self-compassion.

My relationship with self-care has not been easy. I struggled for a long time to find a balance between taking care of myself and taking care of everything else I had on my plate: work, school, family, friends, finances, a sick husband, etc. I share this to tell you that I know and understand that practicing self-care can be hard, because as an Empath you have a huge heart and always want to help those around you. But let me remind you of what my professor said: "Self-care is essential for your survival and well-being." It is not selfish or self-centered. If you don't take care of yourself, you will not be the best version of yourself. You cannot help others or be truly present unless you are well and healthy.

Self-care is not just about taking bubble baths or going shopping (even though those things can be fun). It is more than that—nourishing your body, mind, and soul and making your health and wellness a priority.

As an Empath, you absorb so much of the energy around you and do so much for others. This can leave you feeling depleted, burned out, depressed, angry, resentful, anxious, and stressed. Thus, you must focus on using a holistic approach to your self-care and making it a consistent habit. The main areas where you will want to prioritize self-care include:

- **Physical Self-Care:** Taking care of your body

- **Emotional Self-Care:** Taking care of your heart and managing your emotions

- **Mental Self-Care:** Taking care of your mind and managing your thoughts

- **Spiritual Self-Care:** Connecting with your higher self and honoring your spiritual beliefs

- **Social Self-Care:** Setting clear boundaries, nourishing healthy relationships, and protecting yourself from energy vampires. (Energy vampires are people who drain your energy and leave you depleted. They can be narcissists, those who don't respect your boundaries, nonstop talkers, etc.)

Before you begin, take the Empath Self-Assessment from Dr. Judith Orloff, a psychiatrist and fellow Empath, to better understand your empathic gifts: DrJudithOrloff.com/quizzes/empath-self-assessment-test. And now it's time for you to start your self-care journey. Take what nourishes you, use what restores and replenishes you, and make yourself your number-one priority. Above anything, honor your sensitive soul.

Theme: SPIRITUAL SELF-CARE

I am honored and grateful to be an Empath. I love and accept myself fully.

My Self-Care Goal: I will begin this self-care journey by taking a pledge to fully honor myself and all my empathic gifts.

Each Empath is unique and has special traits and characteristics.

To me, being an Empath means:

_____

_____

_____

_____

_____

_____

_____

_____

_____

_____

_____

_____

_____

_____

_____

_____

_____

_____

_____

_____

My empathic gifts include:

_____

_____

_____

_____

_____

_____

_____

_____

_____

_____

_____

_____

_____

_____

_____

_____

_____

_____

_____

_____

_____

_____

_____

This week, and throughout your self-care journey, set the intention to practice gratitude daily. Begin with this gratitude exercise:

On a separate piece of paper, write down your empathic gifts, your qualities, strengths, and anything else you are grateful for. Then cut out each word, fold it, and place all the words in a jar. This is your gratitude jar. Then every morning, pull out a piece of paper from the jar to remind you what you are grateful for. Keep adding more words to the jar as you wish.

Theme: PHYSICAL SELF-CARE

My body is a fountain of wisdom and strength.

My Self-Care Goal: I will practice listening to and trusting the wisdom of my body.

As an Empath, learning to listen to my body is important.

What is my body telling me?

_____

_____

_____

_____

_____

_____

_____

_____

_____

_____

_____

_____

_____

_____

_____

_____

What is my body asking of me?

_____

_____

_____

_____

_____

_____

_____

_____

_____

_____

_____

_____

How will I respond to my body this week?

_____

_____

_____

_____

_____

_____

_____

_____

_____

_____

_____

_____

The body knows what it needs and what you need. Practice tuning into your body and listening to it. If your body asks you to sleep, sleep; if your body is hungry, feed it; if your body needs to move, move it. Listening to what your body tells you will allow you to better take care of yourself and improve your well-being.

Theme: SPIRITUAL SELF-CARE

I understand that being sensitive is not a flaw, and I fully embrace my gifts and will become who I was born to be.

My Self-Care Goal: Identifying my sensitivities is the first step to honoring and embracing all of who I am. I will honor my sensitivities each day.

Which of these am I sensitive to?

☐ Bright lights

☐ Strong scents

☐ Loud noises

☐ Crowds

☐ Coarse fabrics

☐ Others' emotions, thoughts, or physical pain

☐ Changes in the weather

☐ Changes in the environment

☐ Other: _____

_____

What else am I sensitive to?

_____

_____

_____

_____

_____

_____

_____

_____

_____

_____

_____

_____

_____

_____

_____

_____

_____

_____

_____

_____

_____

How will I honor each of my sensitivities?

_____

_____

_____

_____

_____

_____

_____

_____

_____

_____

_____

_____

Practice mindfulness by paying attention to your sensitivities, accepting them as they are, and allowing them to be. Try not to change them or judge them. Instead, observe them and gently respond to their needs.

For example, "I notice I get overwhelmed by loud noises, so I allow myself quiet time."

Theme: EMOTIONAL SELF-CARE

I feel the pain of those around me, but I don't hold on to it. I release it and say, "This is not my pain; it does not belong to me."

My Self-Care Goal: I will practice separating others' emotions and pain from mine.

Thinking back on the last time I felt overwhelmed by emotions, I ask myself: Was I absorbing these from someone else? Were those feelings mine?

_____

_____

_____

_____

_____

_____

_____

_____

_____

_____

_____

Where were these feelings coming from?

_____

_____

_____

_____

_____

_____

_____

_____

_____

_____

_____

_____

This week, utilize some of the space in this journal to write down the emotions that come to you throughout the day. Try to identify _yours_ vs. _those_ you may have picked up from others.

Allow all the feelings to flow, because emotions need to be felt to be released. Then repeat the affirmation, "I release all that does not belong to me."

Theme: MENTAL SELF-CARE

I am able to manage my thoughts and maintain mental calmness.

My Self-Care Goal: Managing my thoughts and emotions is essential for my well-being and mental health. I will do my best to manage my unhelpful thoughts.

Have I had negative thoughts lately? What are these thoughts and the emotions attached to them?

My thoughts were:

_____

_____

_____

_____

_____

_____

_____

_____

_____

_____

_____

_____

_____

_____

_____

_____

_____

_____

_____

_____

_____

_____

_____

The feelings that came up were:

_____

_____

_____

_____

_____

_____

_____

_____

_____

_____

_____

_____

_____

_____

_____

_____

_____

_____

_____

_____

_____

_____

_____

_____

Challenging unhelpful thoughts can help you maintain a healthier mental state. Use the questions below to help you challenge the thoughts you identified in this week's journal prompt.

Was the thought helpful?

Was the thought accurate?

Is there another way I can think of this?

Theme: SOCIAL SELF-CARE

I protect my energy from those who drain me by setting clear boundaries.

My Self-Care Goal: I will practice expressing my boundaries to those around me.

I recognize the importance of setting and expressing boundaries in my life.

What are some boundaries I need to set?

_____

_____

_____

_____

_____

_____

_____

_____

_____

_____

_____

_____

_____

_____

_____

_____

_____

Who do I need to set boundaries with?

_____

_____

_____

_____

_____

_____

_____

_____

_____

_____

_____

_____

When will I express my boundaries to others?

_____

_____

_____

_____

_____

_____

_____

_____

_____

_____

_____

_____

_____

_____

_____

Boundaries are limits that protect you and keep you safe. It's important to identify who might be an energy vampire for you. This week, identify the boundaries you need to apply in your life and practice expressing them clearly and firmly. Remember that "no" is a complete sentence.

Theme: EMOTIONAL SELF-CARE

I will no longer hold on to people, words, or things that hurt me.

My Self-Care Goal: Even though I am full of empathy, I need to let go of anyone or anything that no longer belongs to me.

Sometimes it is necessary to let go. Knowing what to let go of and when to do that is important.

Are there things in my life that I need to let go of? If so, what?

_____

_____

_____

_____

_____

_____

_____

_____

_____

_____

_____

_____

_____

_____

_____

_____

_____

_____

_____

_____

_____

_____

_____

_____

Are there people in my life that I need to let go of? If so, who?

_____

_____

_____

_____

_____

_____

_____

_____

_____

_____

_____

_____

_____

_____

_____

_____

_____

_____

_____

_____

_____

_____

_____

_____

This week, start practicing the art of letting go by clearing and purging things you no longer use, need, or want. Physically cleansing your space will also help you make space to emotionally let go. Identify who no longer belongs in your life and start the process of letting them go.

Theme: PHYSICAL SELF-CARE

I allow myself to rest, restore, and replenish.

My Self-Care Goal: I will prioritize resting to restore and replenish my energy.

Rest and revitalization are important to me.

How can I make rest a priority and a habit in my life?

_____

_____

_____

_____

_____

_____

_____

_____

_____

_____

_____

_____

_____

_____

_____

_____

_____

_____

_____

_____

What benefits will I get from prioritizing rest?

_____

_____

_____

_____

_____

_____

_____

_____

_____

_____

_____

_____

_____

_____

_____

_____

_____

_____

_____

_____

As an Empath, you are a giver and you love to help others. But you must also remember to pause and rest to prevent burnout.

Choose a few different ways in which you plan to implement rest this week:

- Take naps

- Spend time alone

- Have quiet time

- Take long showers or a bath

- Other: _____

  _____

Theme: SPIRITUAL SELF-CARE

My spirit needs as much nourishment as my body.

My Self-Care Goal: I will take the time to connect with my spirit and ask it what it needs.

Take a moment to be still and listen to your inner voice.

What is my inner voice saying to me? What does my spirit need right now? What spiritual practices bring peace and joy to my soul? What does spiritual health mean to me?

_____

_____

_____

_____

_____

_____

_____

_____

_____

_____

_____

_____

_____

_____

_____

_____

_____

_____

_____

_____

_____

_____

_____

_____

Your spirit needs nourishment every day. Is there a spiritual practice that allows you to connect with yourself on a deeper level? Here are a few exercises to get you started:

- Daily meditation

- Taking deep breaths

- Writing your deepest thoughts, wishes, desires, or fears in your journal

- Spending time in nature

- Burning sage or lighting incense

- Other: _____

_____

Theme: EMOTIONAL SELF-CARE

I allow myself to feel all my emotions and say, "My feelings are valid and deserve that I hold space for them."

My Self-Care Goal: I will make sure I connect with my emotions and not repress them.

Take a moment to tune into your emotions. Place a check next to the ones you identify with:

- ☐ Joyful
- ☐ Peaceful
- ☐ Anxious
- ☐ Stressed
- ☐ Exhausted
- ☐ Energized
- ☐ Happy
- ☐ Sad
- ☐ Angry
- ☐ Hopeful

- ☐ Other: _____

_____

What other emotions have I been experiencing?

_____

_____

_____

_____

_____

_____

_____

_____

_____

_____

_____

_____

_____

_____

_____

_____

_____

_____

Have I been repressing any emotions? If so, what effects, if any, has this suppression had on me?

_____

_____

_____

_____

_____

_____

_____

_____

_____

_____

_____

_____

_____

This week, practice naming your emotions and give them space to be felt. Remember that no feeling is permanent and that repressing a feeling can make it fester. The more you identify and name your emotions, the more you can feel and release them.

Theme: SOCIAL SELF-CARE

I surround myself with positive and encouraging people.

My Self-Care Goal: I will evaluate if I am choosing to be around people who support and encourage me.

Who are the positive people in my life? Describe each person—who they are, how I know them, what they like, what makes them special, etc. These are people who believe in me, share in my joy, and are present in my life.

_____

_____

_____

_____

_____

_____

_____

_____

_____

_____

_____

_____

_____

_____

_____

_____

_____

_____

_____

_____

_____

_____

_____

_____

_____

_____

This week, make it a priority to connect with the people whose names you wrote down as those who are positive people in your life. This can be done via a phone call, texting, or setting up a time to meet with them either virtually or in person. Continue to choose to surround yourself with people who bring you joy and peace.

Theme: MENTAL SELF-CARE

One meditation a day keeps my stress at bay.

My Self-Care Goal: I will find a way to incorporate meditation into my daily routine.

I can meditate by taking a minute of silence, taking a deep breath, or listening to a guided meditation.

In what ways will I meditate this week?

_____

_____

_____

_____

_____

_____

_____

_____

_____

_____

_____

_____

_____

_____

_____

_____

_____

_____

_____

_____

Meditation helps calm the mind, spirit, and nervous system. It also allows us to feel less stressed and to prevent sensory overload. You may use this meditation to start your day (take a look at the Resources section for guided meditation recommendations):

Sit upright in a comfortable chair or on your bed.

Close your eyes and take a deep breath.

Place your right hand on your heart and your left hand on your stomach.

Breathe, inhaling slowly and exhaling with a long sigh (up to 8 seconds long).

Set your intention to start your day with positivity, gratitude, and kindness toward yourself.

Take one last deep breath and close the meditation by saying "I will embrace everything this day brings."

Theme: PHYSICAL SELF-CARE

I set the intention to eat food that is nourishing to me.

My Self-Care Goal: It's important to eat nourishing food every day, and I will explore how to make that a priority and a possibility.

The food I eat can either have a harmful or nourishing effect on my body and spirit.

The food that nourishes my body is:

_____

_____

_____

_____

_____

_____

_____

_____

_____

_____

_____

_____

_____

_____

_____

_____

_____

_____

_____

_____

_____

_____

The food that nourishes my spirit is:

_____

_____

_____

_____

_____

_____

_____

_____

_____

_____

_____

_____

_____

_____

_____

_____

_____

_____

_____

_____

_____

_____

_____

_____

_____

_____

Based on the list of the food you find nourishing to your body and spirit, take yourself shopping and try to get at least three of the items on your list (or more if you are able). For your next meal or snack, eat those foods with intention, taking in the nourishment you receive with each bite.

Theme: SPIRITUAL SELF-CARE

The universe gives me all that I seek and need.

My Self-Care Goal: I deserve to tend to my spiritual self-care and will consider what it is that I want to manifest in my life.

Reaching out for and embracing the energy that the universe provides is important to my daily life.

I ask the energy of the universe for:

_____

_____

_____

_____

_____

_____

_____

_____

_____

_____

_____

_____

_____

_____

_____

_____

_____

_____

_____

_____

_____

_____

_____

I manifest abundance, joy, and peace. I would also like to manifest:

_____

_____

_____

_____

_____

_____

_____

_____

_____

_____

_____

_____

_____

_____

_____

_____

_____

_____

_____

_____

_____

_____

_____

_____

As an Empath, you are connected to the energy of the universe and the universe to you. This week, do your best to trust the flow of positive energy around you and to manifest all that you seek and need.

I focus on my breathing, inhaling deeply and exhaling slowly. I inhale peace. I exhale all negative energy.

My Self-Care Goal: I will take the time to pause, take deep breaths, and self-soothe.

I can use the emotions list below to identify feelings that might need self-soothing:

- Anger
- Anxiety
- Overwhelm
- Fear
- Sadness
- Stress
- Disgust
- Other emotions: _____

_____

_____

_____

What activities help me relax and self-soothe? For example, coloring, squeezing a stress ball, walking, taking a nap, etc.

_____

_____

_____

_____

_____

_____

_____

_____

_____

_____

_____

_____

_____

_____

_____

_____

_____

_____

_____

_____

_____

_____

_____

_____

_____

_____

_____

_____

_____

_____

_____

Deep breathing is a liberating and healing practice for Empaths.
Practice taking deep breaths regularly and when
you need self-soothing in the following way:

1. Inhale through your nose and down into your diaphragm

2. Hold the air in your belly for four seconds

3. Exhale through your mouth for up to seven seconds

4. Repeat 7 to 10 times or until you feel calmer

Theme: SOCIAL SELF-CARE

I have the right to say "no" and to not have to explain myself.

My Self-Care Goal: I will explore where and when I need to say "no" without guilt.

I will say "no" when:

_____

_____

_____

_____

_____

_____

_____

_____

_____

_____

_____

_____

_____

_____

_____

_____

_____

_____

_____

_____

_____

_____

_____

_____

_____

I will say "no" to doing any of the following things:

_____

_____

_____

_____

_____

_____

_____

_____

_____

_____

_____

_____

_____

_____

_____

_____

_____

_____

_____

_____

_____

_____

_____

_____

_____

Empaths love to help and can fall into the habit of people-pleasing. Saying "no" can sometimes be difficult, but it is essential to maintain your balance and protect your energy. Identify when and where you need to say "no" and practice saying it when your inner voice asks you to.

Theme: SPIRITUAL SELF-CARE

Wisdom and love abide in me.

My Self-Care Goal: I will find ways and means to connect with my love and wisdom source.

A form of spiritual self-care is defining what love and wisdom uniquely mean to me.

Love is:

_____

_____

_____

_____

_____

_____

_____

_____

_____

_____

_____

_____

_____

_____

Wisdom is:

_____

_____

_____

_____

_____

_____

_____

_____

_____

_____

_____

_____

_____

_____

_____

_____

How can love and wisdom protect my spirit?

_____

_____

_____

_____

_____

_____

_____

_____

_____

_____

_____

_____

_____

Everyone has their own definition of love and wisdom. Maybe to you, love is a source of energy that comes from within your heart. Perhaps wisdom is the knowledge that your higher self holds that protects and guides you. However, you may define love and wisdom for yourself. This week, allow your love and wisdom to guide you and center you each day.

Theme: PHYSICAL SELF-CARE

My sleep is restorative and reenergizing.

My Self-Care Goal: I will prioritize my sleep and practice sleep hygiene.

Prioritizing sleep and practicing sleep hygiene is important to me.

By prioritizing my sleep, I will get the following benefits:

_____

_____

_____

_____

_____

_____

_____

_____

_____

_____

_____

_____

_____

_____

_____

_____

_____

_____

_____

_____

_____

I can practice sleep hygiene by:

_____

_____

_____

_____

_____

_____

_____

_____

_____

_____

_____

_____

_____

_____

_____

_____

_____

_____

_____

_____

Sleep is essential for Empaths' restoration and reenergizing.

Tips to practice sleep hygiene:

- Put away all devices at least two hours before bedtime
- Avoid eating or drinking at least two hours before bedtime
- Prepare your body for sleep by doing light exercises (e.g., stretching)
- Meditate or practice a spiritual activity to achieve deeper sleep

Theme: MENTAL SELF-CARE

I shield myself with light. Nothing and no one can harm me.

My Self-Care Goal: I acknowledge that there is energy around me everywhere I go. I will protect myself by practicing shielding.

Shielding is a technique that I can use to protect myself from harmful energy—whether it's at work, at home, around family and friends, and especially around energy vampires. When and where do I most need to shield myself?

_____

_____

_____

_____

_____

_____

_____

_____

_____

_____

_____

_____

_____

_____

_____

_____

_____

_____

_____

_____

_____

_____

_____

_____

_____

_____

_____

Practice shielding by using the following visualization recommended by Dr. Judith Orloff:

Imagine a white light shielding your entire body and extending a few inches from you. This light is energy that comes from within you and extends out to protect you. Only positive energy can enter, and no negative energy will be able to penetrate it. Shield yourself anytime you sense heavy or negative energy around you.

Theme: EMOTIONAL SELF-CARE

I give love to myself. I say, "I love you; you are worthy; you are whole."

My Self-Care Goal: Just as I give love and empathy to others, I will give love and empathy to myself.

It is important to speak lovingly to myself.

Write down five positive words to describe myself. (For example, "I am kind, intelligent, funny, loving, and lovable.")

I am:

_____

_____

_____

_____

_____

Using those five positive words as inspiration, use the space here to write a story about something I did recently where I showed myself love and empathy and embodied those five special qualities I identified.

_____

_____

_____

_____

_____

_____

_____

_____

_____

_____

_____

_____

_____

_____

_____

_____

_____

_____

_____

_____

_____

_____

_____

_____

_____

_____

_____

_____

_____

_____

_____

The way you speak to yourself highly impacts your emotional state. Is your internal narrative loving and positive? This week, write a love letter to yourself.

Your letter can include:

- What you like and love about yourself

- What you are proud of

- What you forgive yourself for

- Words of encouragement for the present and future

_____

_____

Theme: SOCIAL SELF-CARE

I will protect myself from people who drain my energy.
I will surround myself with people who nourish me.

My Self-Care Goal: I shall give myself the time and space to identify the relationships that drain me and the ones that nurture me.

It is important to identify people/relationships that drain vs. nurture me.

The people/relationships that drain me include:

_____

_____

_____

_____

_____

_____

_____

_____

_____

_____

_____

_____

_____

_____

_____

_____

_____

_____

_____

_____

_____

_____

The people/relationships that nurture me include:

_____

_____

_____

_____

_____

_____

_____

_____

_____

_____

_____

_____

_____

_____

_____

_____

_____

_____

_____

_____

_____

_____

_____

_____

_____

_____

You have the ability and the power to set boundaries and to choose healthy and nurturing relationships. Empaths tend to attract narcissistic people, so it is essential to be aware of this in order to protect your energy. Practice distancing yourself from people who drain you, and spend more time connecting with those who nourish you.

Theme: EMOTIONAL SELF-CARE

....

I can release stress and negative energy from my body, mind, and soul. I have the power to free myself.

My Self-Care Goal: I will set the intention to release my stress and its negative energy that has been stored within me.

What are the main sources of stress and negativity in my life? (For example, work, narcissists, crowds, loud places, watching the news, social media, etc.)

_____

_____

_____

_____

_____

_____

_____

_____

_____

_____

_____

What coping tools can help me better manage my stress? For example, exercising, journaling, meditating, talking to a friend, going to therapy, etc.

_____

_____

_____

_____

_____

_____

_____

_____

_____

_____

_____

_____

_____

_____

_____

_____

_____

_____

_____

_____

_____

_____

_____

_____

_____

_____

_____

_____

_____

Energy and stress get stored within your entire being. The good news is you can cleanse yourself and release it. First, set the intention to expel all negative energy. Then, practice releasing it through any or all of the following practices:

- Body movement: stretching, yoga, dance, or any way you can move

- Yawning and sighing

- Deep breaths while repeating "I cleanse my energy with each breath."

Theme: SOCIAL SELF-CARE

I have fulfilling and blossoming relationships.

My Self-Care Goal: I will nourish my relationships and continue to grow my positive connections.

Which relationships do I need to nourish?

_____

_____

_____

_____

_____

_____

_____

_____

_____

_____

_____

_____

_____

_____

_____

_____

_____

_____

_____

_____

_____

_____

_____

How will I nourish these relationships?

_____

_____

_____

_____

_____

_____

_____

_____

_____

_____

_____

_____

_____

_____

_____

_____

_____

_____

_____

_____

_____

_____

_____

Tips for nourishing relationships:

- Reach out to check in

- Express love and appreciation

- Use "I" statements when expressing feelings (Example: "I feel joyful when we spend time together", "I feel sad when we don't see each other for a long time.")

- Foster mutual respect and acceptance

- Set gentle yet clear boundaries

Theme: MENTAL SELF-CARE

Growth can be painful but staying stagnant hurts even more.

My Self-Care Goal: I will be brave and vulnerable. I will allow myself to grow and heal even if it hurts.

Identifying areas for growth and for healing are important.

What are some areas in which I still need to grow?

_____

_____

_____

_____

_____

_____

_____

_____

_____

_____

_____

_____

_____

_____

_____

_____

_____

_____

_____

_____

_____

_____

_____

_____

What are some areas in which I still need healing?

_____

_____

_____

_____

_____

_____

_____

_____

_____

_____

_____

_____

_____

_____

_____

_____

_____

_____

_____

_____

_____

_____

_____

_____

_____

_____

Growing and healing take hard work, but it is worth it. Allow yourself enough time to reflect and answer the questions in the prompt. If you feel that you need help, seek support from a therapist, life coach, or spiritual guide.

Mother Nature is my medicine. She nourishes, restores, and heals me.

My Self-Care Goal: I will make it a priority to spend time and connect with nature every week.

Nature is medicine for my body, mind, and spirit.

Using the space below, I will write down at least three activities I will do in nature on a regular basis. (For example, gardening, walks in nature, sunbathing, hugging a tree, etc.)

_____

_____

_____

_____

_____

_____

_____

_____

_____

_____

What about these activities do I enjoy?

_____

_____

_____

_____

_____

_____

_____

_____

_____

_____

_____

_____

_____

_____

_____

_____

_____

_____

_____

_____

What benefits do I get by practicing these activities in nature?

_____

_____

_____

_____

_____

_____

_____

_____

_____

_____

_____

_____

_____

_____

Try to spend as much time as you can in nature. Specifically, try to integrate the technique known as *earthing*. To practice, plant your bare feet on the earth for 10 to 20 minutes or touch the earth with your bare hands. This will allow you to absorb and take in the earth's healing and restorative energy. Take note of how it makes you feel.

Theme: EMOTIONAL SELF-CARE

I release my fear. I connect with my courage and intuitive gifts.

My Self-Care Goal: I will tap into my inner strength and courage. Fear will not hold me back from trusting and following my intuition.

Identifying how fear, courage, and strength appear and impact my life is important to my growth.

My fear has told me:

_____

_____

_____

_____

_____

_____

_____

_____

_____

_____

_____

_____

_____

_____

_____

_____

_____

My courage tells me:

_____

_____

_____

_____

_____

_____

_____

_____

_____

_____

_____

_____

_____

_____

_____

My strengths are:

_____

_____

_____

_____

_____

_____

_____

_____

_____

_____

This week, focus on your strengths and practice trusting and honoring your intuition. When fear sets in, acknowledge it and say, "Thank you for wanting to protect me, but I've got this."

Theme: PHYSICAL SELF-CARE

Just like rain washes away impurities from the earth, water washes away that which burdens me.

My Self-Care Goal: I will replenish and restore my energy in water every day.

Water is life for Empaths because it is revitalizing.

How do I usually feel after being in water (the ocean, a pool, the bathtub, or even a shower)?

_____

_____

_____

_____

_____

_____

_____

_____

_____

_____

_____

_____

_____

_____

_____

_____

_____

_____

_____

What activities can I incorporate in my daily life that center around water?

_____

_____

_____

_____

_____

_____

_____

_____

_____

_____

_____

_____

_____

_____

_____

_____

_____

_____

_____

_____

_____

_____

_____

_____

_____

_____

_____

Practice cleansing your energy in water daily. This can be done by submerging yourself in any body of water, taking a shower, or preferably taking a bath. You can add lavender, Epsom salts, mineral oils, or other herbs for additional calming effects.

Theme: MENTAL SELF-CARE

Whenever I feel overwhelmed, I can go to my safe place.

My Self-Care Goal: I will create a safe and sacred space in my mind, where I can find solace in times of stress.

As a form of mental self-care, I will use the space here to write a description of what my mental safe space looks and feels like. (For example, "In my safe place, I am standing in front of a lake, surrounded by trees. I can feel the wind touch my skin. My safe place is peaceful and bright.")

_____

_____

_____

_____

_____

_____

_____

_____

_____

_____

_____

_____

_____

_____

_____

_____

_____

_____

_____

_____

_____

_____

_____

_____

_____

_____

_____

Every time you feel overwhelmed, visualize your mental safe place and transport yourself there. This is a way to center and ground yourself and connect with your inner peace. Place your hand on your heart and breathe. Repeat the phrase "I am safe and calm."

Theme: PHYSICAL SELF-CARE

I give my brain a break from all work and devices. I protect myself from burnout.

My Self-Care Goal: I will give myself breaks from working and from using the computer, phone, or other electronic devices.

Prioritizing self-care by taking breaks from stimuli is important to me.

What will I take breaks from?

_____

_____

_____

_____

_____

_____

_____

_____

_____

_____

_____

_____

_____

_____

_____

_____

_____

_____

When will I take breaks?

_____

_____

_____

_____

_____

_____

_____

_____

_____

_____

_____

_____

_____

_____

_____

How will I remember to take breaks?

_____

_____

_____

_____

_____

_____

_____

_____

_____

_____

_____

_____

_____

_____

Make a plan to schedule breaks in your daily routine and to
disconnect from all external stimuli, especially from devices.
Allow yourself quiet time and rest to prevent sensory overload
and burnout.

Theme: EMOTIONAL SELF-CARE

Empaths are a gift to a world that needs healing.

My Self-Care Goal: I will practice a deeper appreciation of my empathic gifts and acknowledge how much I have to give.

I am grateful for being an Empath.

What I am able to give to the world includes:

_____

_____

_____

_____

_____

_____

_____

_____

_____

_____

_____

_____

_____

_____

_____

_____

_____

_____

_____

_____

_____

_____

_____

_____

I can make a difference by:

_____

_____

_____

_____

_____

_____

_____

_____

_____

_____

_____

_____

_____

_____

_____

_____

_____

_____

_____

_____

_____

_____

_____

_____

_____

Being an Empath is truly a superpower. Well-known Empaths include Oprah, Princess Diana, Mother Teresa, Nelson Mandela, and Mahatma Gandhi. This week, take the time to reflect on the ways that you, too, can contribute to the greater good.

Theme: EMOTIONAL SELF-CARE

My love language is the language of my heart. I will honor my heart. I will be open to receiving love.

My Self-Care Goal: Although I am a giver by nature and sometimes it may be difficult to receive, I will practice being open to receiving love from others.

How do I express my love to others?

_____

_____

_____

_____

_____

_____

_____

_____

_____

_____

_____

_____

_____

_____

_____

_____

_____

_____

_____

_____

_____

_____

_____

How would I like others to express love to me?

_____

_____

_____

_____

_____

_____

_____

_____

_____

_____

_____

_____

_____

_____

_____

_____

_____

_____

_____

_____

Gary Chapman, author of the book *The 5 Love Languages*, identified five primary ways in which people tend to express and receive love. The five languages are:

- Physical touch

- Giving/Receiving gifts

- Words of affirmation

- Quality time

- Acts of service

Which are your top two love languages?

_____

_____

Theme: MENTAL SELF-CARE

I believe in my ability to choose my own path and make my own decisions.

My Self-Care Goal: I will trust my inner wisdom to guide me each day and when faced with making decisions.

Empaths can sometimes struggle with people-pleasing and self-doubt.

When, if at any time, have I doubted myself and my ability to make decisions?

_____

_____

_____

_____

_____

_____

_____

_____

_____

_____

_____

_____

_____

_____

_____

_____

_____

_____

_____

_____

_____

When was a time that I felt confident to make my own decisions and
trusted my inner wisdom?

_____

_____

_____

_____

_____

_____

_____

_____

_____

_____

_____

_____

_____

_____

_____

_____

_____

_____

_____

_____

_____

_____

_____

_____

_____

_____

_____

This week, think of times when you made wise decisions and followed your instincts. Acknowledge that you already have all you need within you to choose the path that is best for you. Trust yourself and always follow your gut.

Theme: SPIRITUAL SELF-CARE

Music heals and nourishes my soul.

My Self-Care Goal: I will immerse myself in music and allow it to speak to my soul.

What type of music helps calm me down?

_____

_____

_____

_____

_____

_____

_____

_____

_____

_____

_____

_____

_____

_____

_____

_____

_____

_____

_____

_____

_____

_____

_____

_____

Which songs speak to and connect with my soul?

_____

_____

_____

_____

_____

_____

_____

_____

_____

_____

_____

_____

_____

_____

_____

_____

_____

_____

_____

_____

_____

_____

_____

_____

_____

_____

_____

Research shows that music is medicine for the body and the soul. It helps us to heal from emotional and spiritual wounds and can also reduce physical pain. Make it a daily practice to listen to the music that heals you.

Theme: MENTAL SELF-CARE

I can reach my goals and create my own destiny.

My Self-Care Goal: I will visualize the future I want and create a plan to reach my goals.

A goal is something that I want or aspire to achieve. I know that goals require planning and action. Today, I will take some time to identify my goals.

My short-term goals include:

_____

_____

_____

_____

_____

_____

_____

_____

_____

_____

_____

_____

_____

_____

_____

_____

_____

_____

_____

_____

_____

My long-term goals include:

_____

_____

_____

_____

_____

_____

_____

_____

_____

_____

_____

_____

_____

_____

_____

_____

_____

_____

_____

_____

_____

_____

_____

_____

This week, choose one to three goals that you would like to work toward (these could be personal, professional, spiritual, etc.). Think about and then describe—either to a close friend, or in your journal—any actionable steps you will take toward each goal and start by taking the first step. You are an empowered and capable person. Don't let anyone tell you otherwise.

Theme: PHYSICAL SELF-CARE

I will intentionally release any unwanted negative energy stored in my body.

My Self-Care Goal: I will move and/or soothe my body every day to release my unwanted negative energy.

We all experience difficult moments in life, and these can leave a trace in our body and soul. This trace is unwanted negative energy, and it gets stored in the muscles and cells of the body. Thus, when we move and/or soothe our body, it helps to release that energy.

What are some ways I can move my body?

_____

_____

_____

_____

_____

_____

_____

_____

_____

_____

_____

_____

_____

_____

_____

_____

_____

_____

_____

_____

What are some ways I can soothe my body?

_____

_____

_____

_____

_____

_____

_____

_____

_____

_____

_____

_____

_____

_____

_____

_____

_____

_____

_____

The following exercises can help you release unwanted negative energy from your body:

- Yoga

- Massage

- Stretching

- Swimming

- Dance

- Sitting in the shower and allowing the water to stimulate your muscles

- Reiki (performed by a Reiki-certified professional)

Theme: SOCIAL SELF-CARE

I am liberated from the pain and trauma of my ancestors.

My Self-Care Goal: I will no longer hold on to the pain of previous generations. I can have empathy for their suffering, but their pain is not my pain.

My ancestors suffered and/or endured pain in the form of:

_____

_____

_____

_____

_____

_____

_____

_____

_____

_____

_____

_____

_____

_____

_____

_____

_____

_____

_____

_____

_____

_____

I can have empathy, but I will no longer hold on to:

_____

_____

_____

_____

_____

_____

_____

_____

_____

_____

_____

_____

_____

_____

_____

_____

_____

_____

_____

_____

_____

_____

Intergenerational trauma is pain passed on from one generation to the next. You may not realize that you are carrying the pain of your ancestors. Take time to identify any intergenerational trauma that you might be carrying. Write it down on a piece of paper and then destroy the paper—throw it away, shred it, or burn it with the intention of freeing yourself from it.

Theme: SPIRITUAL SELF-CARE

Being sensitive is my superpower.

My Self-Care Goal: I will continue to embrace, honor, and respect my sensitive nature and to acknowledge that it is my biggest strength and asset.

How has being sensitive made me stronger (e.g., in my relationships with myself and others, at work, in my spiritual development, etc.)?

_____

_____

_____

_____

_____

_____

_____

_____

_____

_____

_____

_____

_____

_____

_____

_____

_____

_____

_____

_____

_____

_____

What else makes me strong? Identify at least 3 more of my strengths,
how they manifest, and how they serve me.

_____

_____

_____

_____

_____

_____

_____

_____

_____

_____

_____

_____

_____

_____

_____

_____

_____

_____

_____

_____

_____

_____

_____

_____

_____

On a piece of paper, create a simple drawing of yourself. Write down 8 to 10 words that describe you as an Empath and strong person. Keep this drawing in a place where you can easily see it to remind yourself of your unique strengths when needed.

Theme: EMOTIONAL SELF-CARE

Taking the steps to heal shows strength and courage.

My Self-Care Goal: I will choose to do the work to live less wounded.

Healing is not always linear, and I shouldn't expect it to be immediate.

What goals do I want to set for my own personal healing? (For example, I would like to work on feeling less angry, reduce my anxiety, etc.)

_____

_____

_____

_____

_____

_____

_____

_____

_____

_____

_____

_____

_____

_____

_____

_____

_____

_____

_____

_____

_____

_____

_____

What steps can I take to start or continue my healing process?

_____

_____

_____

_____

_____

_____

_____

_____

_____

_____

_____

_____

_____

_____

_____

_____

_____

Healing takes hard work and can be painful, but doing the work shows courage and strength. The best first step to take is to find a therapist, healer, or coach. You can search for a therapist online, via your insurance, or by asking your primary physician for a referral.

Other ways to work on your healing include:

- Keeping a journal

- Expressing yourself through art, music, or movement

- Spending time with nature and animals

- Talking to someone you trust

- Having a daily spiritual practice

Theme: MENTAL SELF-CARE

My gifts are like a tree that grows and blossoms.

My Self-Care Goal: I will acknowledge that I am growing and continuing to develop my gifts.

To be born as an Empath is a very special gift. My empathic gifts never stop growing.

Which gifts would I like to continue to grow? (For example, listen to my intuition more, listen to my gut feeling about others or about situations, foster my connection with nature and plants, etc.)

_____

_____

_____

_____

_____

_____

_____

_____

_____

_____

How will I make sure I continue to nourish my gifts? For example, practicing them, sharing them with others, writing about them, expressing them through art, etc.

_____

_____

_____

_____

_____

_____

_____

_____

_____

_____

_____

_____

_____

_____

_____

_____

_____

_____

_____

_____

_____

_____

_____

_____

_____

_____

_____

_____

_____

_____

_____

_____

_____

_____

After you've written down which gifts you would like to grow, practice using the gifts intentionally every chance you get. For example, if you'd like to trust your intuition more, you can practice listening to and honoring your inner voice. You can also continue to grow and nourish your gifts by writing about them, talking to other Empaths, sharing your gifts with others, and expressing them using your creativity (music, art, sculpting, etc).

Theme: PHYSICAL SELF-CARE

I love and accept my body. My body is full of life and beauty.

My Self-Care Goal: I will set the intention to speak to my body with love and gentleness.

Complete the following sentences:

Dear body, thank you for:

_____

_____

_____

_____

_____

_____

_____

_____

_____

_____

_____

_____

_____

_____

_____

_____

I love you because:

_____

_____

_____

_____

_____

_____

_____

_____

_____

_____

_____

_____

_____

My favorite parts of my body are:

_____

_____

_____

_____

_____

_____

_____

_____

_____

_____

_____

_____

Practice speaking to your body each day with love and
gratitude. Thank your body for breathing, for waking up
another day, and for its life, wisdom, and beauty. Treat your body
with loving kindness by using lotions, essential oils, taking a
bath, or enjoying a spa day if possible (either at a professional
place or at home).

Theme: SOCIAL SELF-CARE

I don't take what others say or do personally, because I know that I am not responsible for others' words or actions.

My Self-Care Goal: I will work on not taking the things others say or do personally.

When was the last time I took something personally?

_____

_____

_____

_____

_____

_____

_____

_____

_____

_____

_____

_____

_____

_____

_____

_____

_____

_____

What was it, and how did I feel about it?

_____

_____

_____

_____

_____

_____

_____

_____

_____

_____

_____

_____

_____

_____

_____

When did I realize that I wasn't responsible for it?

_____

_____

_____

_____

_____

_____

_____

_____

_____

_____

_____

_____

When someone says something hurtful, rude, or upsetting to you, take a pause, breathe, and think before you react. Acknowledge that the person has their own emotions and perspective, and they will make their own decisions. If there is anything you need to own, do it, and let the rest go. You are not responsible for their actions or emotions.

Theme: SPIRITUAL SELF-CARE

I find balance and harmony by connecting with the energy of the elements of the Earth.

My Self-Care Goal: I will connect with the elements of air, water, earth, and fire.

In the space below, I will write about ways in which I can best connect to the different elements.

I can connect with air by taking walks outdoors, observing the breeze and wind, feeling the air against my skin, smelling it, sensing it.

This week, I will connect with the element of air in the following ways:

_____

_____

_____

_____

_____

_____

_____

_____

I can connect with water by taking baths, showers, swimming, going in the ocean, etc.

This week, I will connect with the element of water in the following ways:

_____

_____

_____

_____

_____

_____

_____

I can connect with the earth by touching the ground with my bare hands and feet, gardening, etc.

This week, I will connect with the element of earth in the following ways:

_____

_____

_____

_____

_____

_____

_____

_____

_____

I can connect with fire by lighting a candle, burning incense, sitting next to a fire pit or fireplace, etc.

This week, I will connect with the element of fire in the following ways:

_____

_____

_____

_____

_____

_____

_____

_____

Each one of the elements of the Earth has a healing benefit. Through them you are restored, cleansed, grounded, and can find inner and outer balance that is often lost to the noise that surrounds you. Make it a daily part of your routine to connect with the elements. You'll likely find that you live much happier and in harmony.

Theme: EMOTIONAL SELF-CARE

I am full of peace and tranquility. I let go of all stress and anxiety.

My Self-Care Goal: I will work on letting go of my stress and anxiety and practice radical acceptance.

Sometimes I hold on to stress and anxiety because they give me a false sense of feeling in control of my emotions and/or surroundings.

Am I holding on to my stress and anxiety? If so, is there anything I need to work on accepting? Is there anything I need to let go control of?

_____

_____

_____

_____

_____

_____

_____

_____

_____

_____

_____

_____

_____

_____

_____

_____

_____

_____

_____

_____

_____

_____

_____

_____

_____

_____

One of the best ways to combat stress and anxiety is by practicing radical acceptance. Radical acceptance teaches you to accept life as it comes and to embrace what is outside of your control. The more you resist it, the more you suffer. The more you accept it, the more peace you have. Make radical acceptance a practice in your life.

Theme: MENTAL SELF-CARE

I am creative, innovative, and intelligent.

My Self-Care Goal: I will further tap into my creativity and ability to innovate.

One way to tend to my mental self-care is to identify at least three ways in which I demonstrate creativity and innovation. (For example, I have a beautiful singing voice; I am an entrepreneur; I am great at creating new cooking recipes.)

_____

_____

_____

_____

_____

_____

_____

_____

_____

_____

_____

_____

_____

_____

_____

_____

_____

_____

_____

_____

Describe how I will foster each one of my talents. (For example, I will sing daily, I will work on my business plan, I will practice creating new recipes.)

_____

_____

_____

_____

_____

_____

_____

_____

_____

_____

_____

_____

_____

_____

_____

_____

_____

_____

_____

_____

_____

_____

Empaths are incredibly creative; they are pioneers in what they do. This week, foster this side of you by practicing the activities in which you show creativity. For example, if you are a talented singer, sing; if you are a gifted writer, write; if you are a daring artist, create.

Theme: SOCIAL SELF-CARE

Being an Empath allows me to have deep and meaningful relationships.

My Self-Care Goal: I will trust my ability to build meaningful relationships.

How can my intuition and my empathic gifts help my relationships?

_____

_____

_____

_____

_____

_____

_____

_____

_____

_____

_____

_____

_____

_____

_____

_____

_____

_____

_____

_____

_____

_____

_____

_____

_____

What steps can I take to continue to deepen my relationships?

_____

_____

_____

_____

_____

_____

_____

_____

_____

_____

_____

_____

_____

_____

_____

_____

_____

_____

_____

_____

_____

_____

_____

_____

_____

As an Empath, you have the special gift of emotionally sensing and understanding those around you. When you trust this gift and intuitively respond to it, it will allow you to deepen and improve your relationships. For example, if you sense that a friend is in pain and you have the energy for it, you can reach out and offer to provide support.

Theme: SPIRITUAL SELF-CARE

I connect with my ancestors by practicing the beautiful and rich traditions they passed on to me.

My Self-Care Goal: I will practice the traditions that bring me joy and help me connect with my ancestors.

What are some traditions passed on by my parents, grandparents, great-grandparents, individuals identified as family to me, or my caregivers?

_____

_____

_____

_____

_____

_____

_____

_____

_____

_____

_____

_____

Which traditions would I like to continue practicing and passing on?

_____

_____

_____

_____

_____

_____

_____

_____

_____

_____

_____

_____

_____

_____

_____

_____

_____

_____

_____

This week, incorporate the ancestral traditions you identified into your daily routine. Maybe you learned a recipe from your grandmother, so you could take the time to cook this meal and share it with others. Connecting with your ancestors allows you to connect deeper with yourself and the universe.

I am grounded and centered. Overwhelm has no room in my life.

My Self-Care Goal: I will identify my stressors without allowing them to take over my life and practice grounding myself daily.

The main sources of my stress are:

_____

_____

_____

_____

_____

_____

_____

_____

_____

_____

_____

_____

_____

_____

_____

_____

_____

_____

_____

_____

_____

_____

What are areas in which I can ask for help or support?

_____

_____

_____

_____

_____

_____

_____

_____

_____

_____

Is there anything on my to-do list I can eliminate? I should prioritize and remember to take breaks each day to ground myself.

_____

_____

_____

_____

_____

_____

_____

_____

_____

Practice grounding yourself with the following exercise:

- Name five things you can see

- Identify four things you can touch

- Identify three things you can hear

- Find two things you can smell

- Find one thing you can taste

You can also ground yourself by taking deep breaths, meditating, taking quiet time, connecting with nature, and focusing on one thing at a time to prevent sensory overload.

Theme: SOCIAL SELF-CARE

Sometimes I need to say "no" to others in order to say "yes" to myself.

My Self-Care Goal: Grant myself permission to say "yes" to what I need and "no" to what I cannot or do not want to do.

Establishing boundaries is healthy and necessary. It is equally important to identify where and what I can use more of in life.

Identify areas where I can give more to myself. (For example, more free time, more fun time, more alone time, etc.)

_____

_____

_____

_____

_____

_____

_____

_____

_____

_____

_____

_____

_____

_____

_____

_____

_____

_____

_____

_____

_____

Identify areas where I can set better boundaries. (For example, not answering emails or texts right away, saying no to activities I don't enjoy, etc.)

_____

_____

_____

_____

_____

_____

_____

_____

_____

_____

_____

_____

_____

_____

_____

_____

_____

_____

_____

_____

_____

_____

_____

_____

_____

Sometimes when you give so much to others, it keeps you from taking care of yourself. It's important to remember to put yourself first. This week, practice giving yourself more and enjoy the simple pleasures in life, such as a cup of tea, water with lemon, a favorite snack, a nap, smelling the flowers in nature, etc.

Theme: SOCIAL SELF-CARE

Being told I am "too sensitive" will no longer hurt me; instead, I feel empowered by knowing this is a gift that I have.

My Self-Care Goal: When others tell me that I'm too sensitive, I will not be offended but instead will take it as a compliment.

When have I been told I'm too sensitive? What memories do I have of these moments, and how have they affected me?

_____

_____

_____

_____

_____

_____

_____

_____

_____

_____

_____

_____

_____

_____

_____

_____

_____

_____

_____

_____

_____

_____

_____

_____

_____

Practice your boundaries by not engaging or reacting when others say something hurtful such as "You are too sensitive." When you react to those comments, you give away your power, but by remaining calm you take your power back.

Some responses you could use include:

- "Thank you for acknowledging that."

- "I know, you're right. I am sensitive."

I practice self-awareness by noticing my thoughts, emotions, and behaviors.

My Self-Care Goal: I will make the time to self-reflect and self-evaluate.

Keeping track of my thoughts, emotions, and behaviors can help me break unhealthy patterns. Below is an example:

Situation/ Trigger	*My sibling forgot my birthday.*
Thoughts	*They don't care enough about me.*
Emotions	*Sad, angry, hurt.*
Behaviors	*Cried, stayed in bed for a day.*
Alternative Thinking	*They might have been tied up with work duties and didn't have the opportunity to reach out.*

Use the following thought tracker to help you track and challenge
negative or unhelpful thoughts, emotions, and behaviors.

Situation/ Trigger	
Thoughts	
Emotions	
Behaviors	
Alternative Thinking	

What did the thought tracker teach me about self-awareness?

_____

_____

_____

_____

_____

_____

_____

_____

_____

_____

_____

_____

_____

_____

Self-awareness is emotional gold. It is the key to growth and change. Practice increasing your self-awareness by keeping track of your thought/emotion/behavior patterns. You can do this by using the thought tracker in this week's prompt and/or by taking moments to evaluate yourself and reflect.

Theme: PHYSICAL SELF-CARE

My body, mind, and soul are in alignment and harmony with each other.

My Self-Care Goal: I will practice a holistic approach to my self-care for the wellness of my entire being.

I take care of my body by:

_____

_____

_____

_____

_____

_____

_____

_____

_____

_____

_____

_____

_____

_____

_____

_____

_____

I take care of my mind by:

_____

_____

_____

_____

_____

_____

_____

_____

_____

_____

_____

_____

_____

_____

I take care of my soul by:

_____

_____

_____

_____

_____

_____

_____

_____

_____

_____

_____

_____

_____

Make a list of your favorite self-care practices learned in this journal. Keep the list somewhere visible and remind yourself to keep practicing your daily self-care activities. Each day, repeat the phrase "There is nothing more important than taking care of me."

WEEK 52

Theme: EMOTIONAL SELF-CARE

I am a blossoming and thriving Empath. I will live a life of abundance and happiness.

My Self-Care Goal: I will allow myself to experience joy and recognize my growth each day.

In what ways have I grown as an Empath?

What have been some of the greatest lessons and realizations I've had through my self-care journey this year?

_____

_____

_____

_____

_____

_____

_____

_____

_____

_____

_____

_____

_____

_____

_____

_____

_____

_____

_____

_____

_____

_____

_____

_____

_____

_____

_____

_____

_____

_____

_____

To continue to take care of and honor yourself, practice the following visualization:

1. Sit or lie down comfortably

2. Close your eyes and take a deep breath

3. Visualize yourself standing in front of you—you are beautiful, radiant, and flawless. You are free of all pain and fear. There is nothing holding you back

4. This is your higher self, and they already exist and live within you

5. Allow yourself to experience joy and to live each day as your higher self

Resources

HOW TO FIND A THERAPIST

Some of the exercises in this journal may bring up unhealed wounds for you, and if you experience this, it is important for you to have a safe space to process and heal. Finding the right therapist can make all the difference in your healing and transformational journey.

You can find a therapist by taking one of the following steps:

- Ask your doctor or insurance for a referral

- Search the following therapist directories:

  PsychologyToday.com   CliniciansOfColor.org
  LatinxTherapy.com   OpenPathCollective.org
  TherapyForBlackGirls.com

- Call a nonprofit or community mental health center in your area

BOOKS

***The Happy Empath: A Survival Guide for Highly Sensitive People* by Christine Rose Elle**

High sensitivity can be a valuable gift, and this guide will help you harness and strengthen your skills as an Empath while reducing stress and distraction. From the office to home and even online, you'll learn to protect yourself in 19 different everyday environments—and deepen your relationships with those you encounter.

***The Empath's Workbook: Practical Strategies for Nurturing Your Unique Gifts and Living an Empowered Life* by Krista Carpenter MS**

Being an Empath is like having a superpower, but the ability to take on other people's emotions can also be overwhelming. *The Empath's Workbook* will help you gain more control over what you feel and teach you how to develop your intuitive gifts with insightful advice, guided exercises, and self-exploration.

WEBSITES

HSPerson.com

Empaths share many of the same traits with highly sensitive people (HSPs), such as being sensitive to bright lights, strong smells, crowds, loud noises, etc. This website provides resources to help HSPs better cope and manage their sensitivities, as well as valuable research information by Dr. Elaine N. Aron, to better understand what it means to be an HSP.

DrJudithOrloff.com

Dr. Judith Orloff is a psychiatrist, an intuitive healer, and fellow Empath. This website includes many resources, videos, quizzes, and a blog to help Empaths improve their emotional health.
You can also take the Empath's self-assessment on this site (DrJudithOrloff.com/quizzes/empath-self-assessment-test) to better explore and understand your gifts.

ARTICLES

"5 Scientific Explanations of Empathy and Empaths" by Judith Orloff, MD

A great and concise article by Dr. Orloff on the scientific explanations of Empaths, such as the mirror neuron system, electromagnetic fields, emotional contagion, etc. A very easy read that will give you a deeper insight on the science behind being an Empath. Chopra.com/articles /5-scientific-explanations-of-empathy-and-empaths.

"Empowered by Sensitivity: What Type of Empath Are You?" by Aletheia Luna

There are more than seven different types of Empaths according to researchers. Read this article (LonerWolf.com/what-type-of -empath-are-you) to discover the different types of Empaths and help you better identify what type of Empath you are. You can also take a self-test to better assist you in identifying your type.

MEDITATION APPS

Daily meditation is essential for maintaining a calm nervous system and managing stress. This is one of the most important self-care practices for Empaths. Some of my favorite apps for meditation are:

- *Insight Timer:* InsightTimer.com

- *Calm:* Calm.com

- *UCLA Mindful:* UCLAHealth.org/marc/ucla-mindful-app

- *Liberate:* LiberateMeditation.com

ADDITIONAL RESOURCES

I have spent many years collecting resources and creating my own. You can find more resources for Empaths on my professional website KimballTherapy.com/mentalhealthresources.

References

Aron, Elaine. 2016. *The Highly Sensitive Person: How to Thrive When the World Overwhelms You.* New York: Harmony Books.

Chapman, Gary D. 2015. *The 5 Love Languages: The Secret to Love That Lasts.* Chicago: Northfield Pub.

Levine, Peter A. 2008. *Healing Trauma: A Pioneering Program for Restoring the Wisdom of Your Body.* Boulder, CO: Sounds True.

Luna, Aletheia. 2012. *Empowered by Sensitivity: What Type of Empath Are You?* Retrieved from: LonerWolf.com/what-type-of-empath -are-you.

Orloff, Judith. 2017. *The Empath's Survival Guide: Life Strategies for Sensitive People.* Boulder, CO: Sounds True.

Orloff, Judith. 2021. *Are You an Empath? 20 Question Self-Assessment Test.* Retrieved from: DrJudithOrloff.com/quizzes/empath-self -assessment-test.

Van der Kolk, Bessel A. 2015. *The Body Keeps the Score: Brain, Mind, and Body in the Healing of Trauma.* New York: Penguin Books.

ACKNOWLEDGMENTS

I wish to thank God for the gift of my life and for giving me an abundance of opportunities. Thank you to my husband, Paul, and my parents, Gloria and Ricardo, for their love and sacrifices and for always believing in me.

Thank you to my grandfather, Dr. Carlos Marin Arcia, for being an exemplary and loving Empath and for guiding me each day. Thank you to my sister, Gloria, my aunt Shirley, my best friend, Irella, my godson, Carlos Alexis, and to everyone who has supported me on my path. Last but not least, thank you to my clients, for the honor of letting me be their therapist.

ABOUT THE AUTHOR

 **Mishka Clavijo Kimball** is a Latina licensed marriage and family therapist, life coach, professor, and founder of Kimball Therapy and Kimball Collective LLC. She is also an Intuitive, Emotional, and Physical Empath. She specializes in helping highly sensitive adults and Empaths going through life transitions, experiencing anxiety, depression, and grief. Her mission is to help others heal and transform from the inside out. She has a master's of science in counseling psychology and a bachelor of arts in psychology. She is also a certified anger management counselor.

Mishka has years of experience working as a mental health professional and helping make a difference in her community. She has been featured on news outlets and television shows on networks such as LATV, Fox Los Angeles, and Univision.

CPSIA information can be obtained
at www.ICGtesting.com
Printed in the USA
JSHW051739281221
21607JS00001B/1